Water and Fiber
for a Healthy Body

Angela Royston

Heinemann Library
Chicago, Illinois

©Heinemann Library
a division of Capstone Global Library LLC
Chicago, Illinois

Customer Service   888–454–2279

Visit our website at www.heinemannraintree.com

Printed and bound in China by CTPS

13 12 11 10 09
10 9 8 7 6 5 4 3 2 1

Library of Congress Cataloging-in-Publication Data
Royston, Angela.
  Water and fiber for a healthy body / Angela Royston.
    p. cm. -- (Body needs)
  Summary: Discusses what water and fiber are, what foods they can be found in, and how the body absorbs, digests and uses these ingredients.
  Includes bibliographical references and index.
  ISBN 978 1 432921 90 3 (hb)
  ISBN 978 1 432921 96 5 (pb)
  1. Water in the body--Juvenile literature. 2. Fiber in human nutrition--Juvenile literature. [1. Water in the body. 2. Fiber in human nutrition. 3. Nutrition.] I. Title. II. Series.
  QP535.H1R695 2003
  612.3'923--dc21

612.3
ROY

                                    2002012684

Acknowledgments
We would like to thank the following for permission to reproduce photographs: ©Corbis: pp. **8**, **15**, **22**, **27**, **28** (Sygma/Jean Pierre), **30**, **33**; ©Gareth Boden: pp. **5**, **6**, **12**, **34**, **40**, **41**; ©Liz Eddison: pp. **9**, **14**, **39**, **42**; ©Photodisc: pp. **38**; ©Photolibrary Group Ltd: pp. **7** (Imagestate RM/Foodfolio Foodfolio), **10** (Fancy/Tomas Rodriguez), **29** (Radius Images), **32** (Fresh Food Images/Roger Stowell); ©SPL: pp. **18** (Eye of Science), **19** (Biophoto Associates), **31**, **35** (CNRI); ©Trevor Clifford: p. **24**; ©USDA Center for Nutrition Policy and Promotion p. **37**.

Cover photograph of red apple being peeled, reproduced with permission of ©PhotoLibrary Group/Foodpix/Burke/Triolo Productions.

We would like to thank Dr. Sarah Schenker and Nicole A. Clark for their invaluable assistance in the preparation of this book.

Every effort has been made to contact copyright holders of any material reproduced in this book. Any omissions will be rectified in subsequent printings if notice is given to the publishers.

Contents

Any words appearing in the text in bold, **like this**, are explained
in the glossary.

Why Do We Need to Eat?

You need to eat and drink to stay alive. All of the food you eat contains **nutrients**, which your body uses to get **energy**, to grow new **cells**, and to get the chemicals it needs to work properly. If your body lacks nutrients, you will become sick.

Nutrients

Nutrients are divided into groups, according to what they supply. **Carbohydrates** and **fats** supply energy. **Proteins** supply **amino acids**, which are the building blocks needed to make new cells and repair old cells. **Vitamins** and **minerals** supply chemicals that the cells need to function properly. Most foods contain a mixture of nutrients, but many are particularly rich in one kind.

Energy foods

Your body uses energy all the time. Running, walking, and activities that involve moving around use up more energy than quieter activities, such as thinking, eating, and breathing, but even sleeping uses up some energy. Most of your energy comes from the carbohydrates and fats that you eat. Carbohydrates include potatoes, rice, and food made from wheat, such as bread and pasta. Sugar is also a carbohydrate, so cookies, cakes, and candies all give you energy. But the energy from these foods does not last long.

Fats

Fats come from animals and from plants. Butter, milk, and cheese contain quite a lot of animal fat, while margarines and oils are made from plants. The body stores any extra fat you eat as a layer of fat under the skin and within the body.

YOU ARE WHAT YOU EAT

Your body is composed of the same kind of nutrients that you eat. Muscles are mainly protein, while your bones contain the minerals calcium and phosphorus. Under your skin is a layer of fat that helps to keep you warm.

Proteins

Much of your body is made of protein, so, as old cells wear out and die, the body needs constant supplies of new protein to build new cells. While you are still growing, your body needs extra protein to create millions of extra cells. Meat, fish, milk, and beans are all good sources of protein.

This family is enjoying a meal that is rich in nutrients. Although we say they are enjoying spaghetti with meat sauce, they are really taking in carbohydrates with protein and vitamin sauce.

Vitamins and minerals

Most foods contain small amounts of vitamins and minerals. Minerals include **zinc**, **calcium**, **iron**, and **phosphorus**. Fruits and vegetables contain several vitamins and minerals. Milk and cheese contain different ones. Your body only needs small amounts of these chemicals, so, as long as you eat a wide range of foods in adequate amounts, you will get all the vitamins and minerals you need.

Water and Fiber

We usually think of healthy food as food that contains plenty of nutrients, but this book looks at two essential ingredients that are not nutrients: water and fiber. They are not nutrients because they do not supply energy or help the growth of new cells, and they do not contain vitamins and minerals that the cells need to function. However, water in particular is essential for us to live, and fiber is necessary to help keep the bowels healthy.

Water

Up to 60 percent of your body is water. Body fluids like blood, **urine**, digestive juices, and **mucus** are all mainly water. But all cells contain water, so even the parts of the body that look solid, such as muscles, skin, and other **organs**, contain water, too.

Losing water

Your body is losing water all the time, mainly through urine and sweat. You need to take in clean water to replace the water that is lost every day. If you do not drink enough, you can become **dehydrated**. A person can survive for several weeks without food, but your body quickly becomes dehydrated and you would die after a few days without water.

Body fact

If you weigh 42 kilograms (93 pounds), about 28 kilograms (62 pounds) of that is made up of water. This means that your body contains about 28 liters (59 pints) of water.

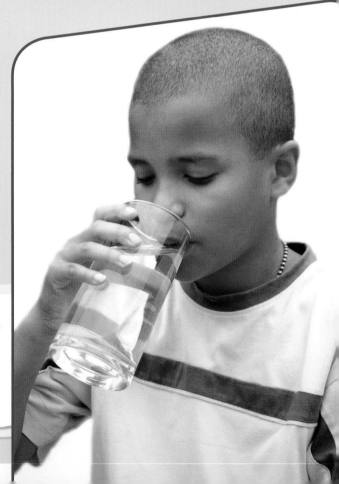

>> Drinking plain water is the best way to take in water, but most drinks and many foods contain water, too.

Fiber

Fiber is the parts of plants that your body cannot **digest**. It consists mainly of the hard walls of plant cells. At one time people thought that fiber was simply waste that the body could do without, but then scientists realized that fiber is needed to keep the digestive system healthy and working well. Fiber helps the body to get rid of **feces** more quickly.

The digestive system

The digestive system breaks up food into pieces that are small enough so that the nutrients in the food can pass into the blood. Most digestion takes place in the **small intestine**. Any food components that are not digested pass through the **large intestine** and collect at the end. They are expelled from your body through the anus when you go to the bathroom.

Getting rid of waste

Both water and fiber are important in getting rid of waste. Feces are easier to expel if they are moist and soft. Fiber absorbs water and so makes the feces bulkier and softer.

Eating an orange is a good way of taking in fiber and liquid. The drops of orange juice are held together by a thin film, or membrane. The membrane is fiber that is not digested.

What Is Water?

Water is made up of just two **elements**—**hydrogen** and **oxygen**—combined together. Both of these elements are normally gases, but when they combine together, they form a liquid. Many substances **dissolve** easily in water, and so water usually contains other chemicals, too. Some of these chemicals are minerals that your body can use. In contaminated water there are **bacteria** and **pollutants** that cause harm.

Calcium in water

Some water contains a lot of calcium. Calcium is a mineral that makes your bones and teeth strong. The disadvantage is that it makes the water "hard" and leaves a hard, chalky-white deposit in kettles and in pipes. It takes more soap to get a lather in hard water.

Bacteria in water

Bacteria, like many forms of life, need water to live and breed. Typhoid, cholera, and dysentery are three serious illnesses that are carried by water. They are caused by bacteria and kill thousands of people every year. The water you drink must be treated to kill bacteria, and this treatment makes it safe to drink.

Tap water

The water that comes out of your faucets has been treated before it is piped to homes and other buildings. The **sediments** are filtered out of the water. A chemical called chlorine is added to kill any bacteria. In some places the mineral fluoride is added, too. Fluoride can help protect your teeth from tooth decay and it is also added to most toothpastes.

 Water is treated to make it safe to drink before it is sent to your home.

Water filters

Some people do not like the taste of tap water. Water filters reduce the amount of calcium and chlorine in the water. Some people think that this makes the water "softer" and that it tastes better, too.

Bottled water

Some companies produce bottled water that has been collected from underground springs. Many people think that bottled water tastes better than tap water. However, bottled water is expensive, and many people consider it an unnecessary luxury.

 This jug contains a water filter. It is used to filter tap water.

Water fact

The water you drink is the same water that the dinosaurs drank! Earth's water is constantly **recycled**. It **evaporates** from the oceans and falls as rain. Some of the rain runs into reservoirs, wells, and underground springs. The rest flows into rivers and back to the oceans.

Water in Food

Even solid foods contain a lot of water. This is because all food comes from plants, **fungi**, or animals. Like all living things, they consist mainly of water. Some foods contain more water than others. Leafy vegetables, such as lettuce, have the most—they are over 90 percent water.

Plants

Plants take in water from the soil through their roots. Dissolved in the water are nutrients that the plant needs to remain healthy. The water and nutrients travel through narrow tubes up the stem to the leaves. Here, some of the water combines with **carbon dioxide** from the air to make food, using the energy of sunlight. The sugary food is carried to all other parts of the plant — the flowers, fruit, stem, leaves, and roots.

Fruit juice

Fruit contains seeds that can grow into new plants. Some plants surround the seeds with sweet, juicy flesh. This kind of fruit contains a lot of water and is often made into fruit juice. The fruit of apples, oranges, pineapples, peaches, and mangoes, for example, are crushed, and the juice is collected and sold in bottles or cartons.

VEGETABLE OR FRUIT?

Although we think of cucumbers, eggplant, peppers, and tomatoes as vegetables, they are really fruits. You can see the seeds inside them.

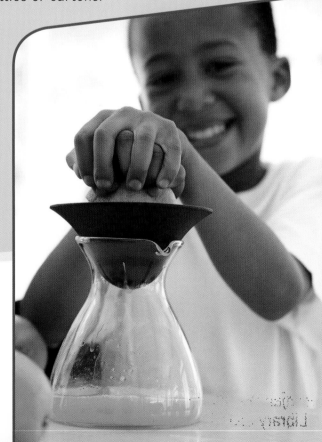

You can squeeze oranges to make orange juice. When the squeezing has finished, the only solids left will be the skin, the pith, and the seeds.

Other food from plants

Nuts, grains, peas, and beans are seeds, too. They contain water, but not as much as juicy fruits. Most vegetables come from other parts of the plant, and they are all rich in water. Cabbage, watercress, and lettuce are leaves and contain the most water. Broccoli and cauliflowers are flowers, while celery and asparagus are stems. Some plants store food in their roots. Potatoes and onions are two examples of root vegetables. Some vegetables, such as carrots, are juiced and sold as drinks.

Food from animals

Meat and fish are more than half water, but meat contains much less water than fruits and vegetables. Female cows, sheep, and goats make milk that we drink or make into cheese and yogurt. Milk is about 90 percent water, so when you have a drink of milk you are drinking mainly water. The other 10 percent consists of fat, sugar, and protein, as well as vitamins and minerals.

Dried food

Sometimes food is dried to preserve it. For example, raisins are a kind of dried grape. Even so, they still contain some water. Dried dates are 15 percent water.

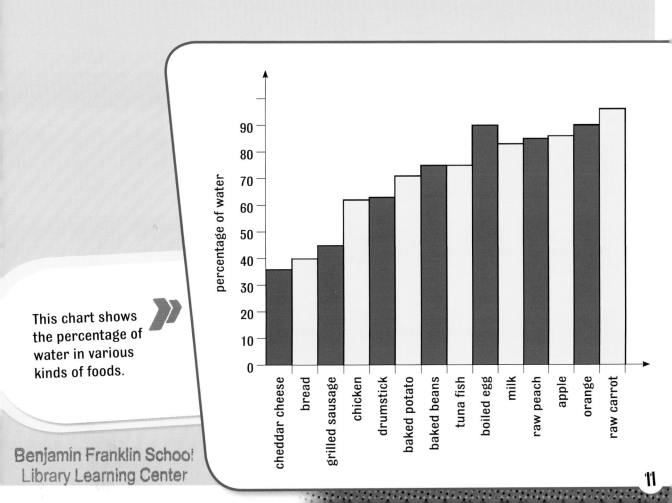

This chart shows the percentage of water in various kinds of foods.

What Is Fiber?

"Fiber" is the term given to a mixture of substances, mainly complex carbohydrates. These cannot be digested in the small intestine in humans, but pass into the large intestine, where they are **fermented**. Fiber can be classified as **insoluble**, such as **cellulose**, or **soluble**, such as pectin, depending on whether or not it dissolves in ethanol (a type of alcohol).

Insoluble fiber

Cellulose is a strong, rubbery material that forms the walls of all the cells that make up a plant. Leaves, stems, flowers, fruits, and roots all contain cellulose. Plant cells are too small to see and so you cannot see all the fiber in a plant, but some plants contain hard or stringy parts that are easy to see. Celery and rhubarb, for example, are stems, and they have stringy pieces that run from one end to the other. Seeds, particularly beans and grains, are often protected with a tough outer skin that is rich in cellulose. The skin of an apple, for example, or of a potato contains more fiber than the rest of it.

Digesting cellulose

Cellulose is a carbohydrate that cows, sheep, and other grazing animals can digest. Humans, however, cannot digest cellulose because the human digestive system does not contain the **enzymes** that are needed to break it down. This means that although fiber is mainly carbohydrate, eating it does not give you any energy.

》 When you cut up scarlet runner beans, you can easily see the stringy fibers that give the beans their strength. But the tough skin that covers fava beans (also shown here) contains cellulose, too.

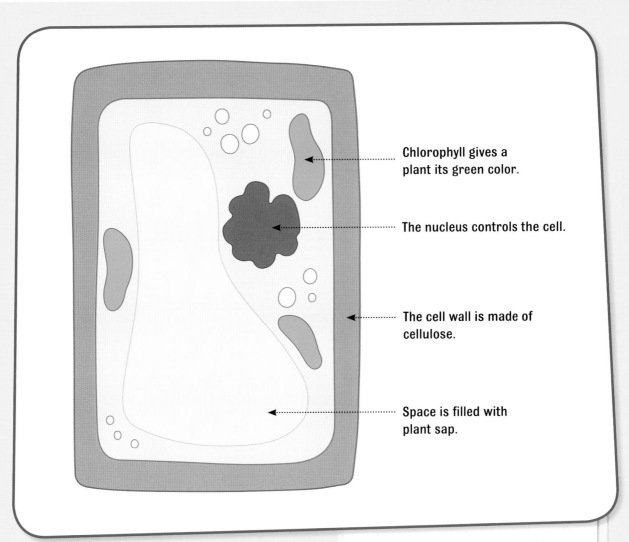

Chlorophyll gives a plant its green color.

The nucleus controls the cell.

The cell wall is made of cellulose.

Space is filled with plant sap.

The walls of plant cells are made of cellulose. Some parts of the plant have thick cell walls containing extra cellulose.

Chewing

Cellulose is very tough, so it is difficult to chew. It takes longer, for example, to chew up a mouthful of raw carrot than it does to chew a piece of chocolate. After chewing, you also have more to swallow. Chewing helps your digestive system because it breaks up the food into smaller pieces before you swallow it, making it easier to digest. In addition, the more you chew, the more **saliva** your mouth makes, and saliva contains an enzyme that starts to digest other carbohydrates.

Soluble fiber

Soluble fiber includes pectins and gums found in fruits, such as apples, and vegetables, such as turnips and sweet potatoes. It is also present in oats. Soluble fiber in the diet can help to reduce the amount of **cholesterol** in the blood.

Fiber in Food

Although you can clearly see stringy pieces in many vegetables, the foods that are richest in fiber are nuts, dried fruit, beans, lentils, and peas. Foods made from grains, such as rice and wheat, which are made into bread and pasta, are also full of fiber. Rice and wheat, however, are often processed so that most of the fiber is taken out of them. This is called refining.

Nuts and dried fruit

Nuts are the seeds of some trees. They include coconuts, hazelnuts, walnuts, almonds, and pine nuts. Nuts are rich in fiber, protein, and oils, which are a kind of fat. Dried fruits include dates, prunes, and desiccated (dried out) coconut. Raisins, sultanas, and currants are all different types of dried grapes.

Pulses

Pulses are seeds from pods, such as beans, lentils, and peas, and are rich in protein as well as in fiber. Other pulses are made into tasty dishes. The Indian food dahl is made from lentils mixed with spices, and the dip hummus is made mainly from chickpeas.

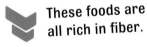
These foods are all rich in fiber.

In many countries, grains are ground by hand. This means that all of the grain is used, and the flour is full of nutrients and fiber.

Grains

Grains come from cereal crops, such as wheat, rice, oats, maize, and barley. Breakfast cereals, as the name suggests, are made from cereal grains. The grains we eat most are wheat and rice. Wheat is ground into flour that is used to make bread, pasta, cakes, and cookies. Rice is normally eaten as a grain with meat or vegetables. How much fiber we get from grains depends on how much of the grain is used in the food. Brown rice and whole grain foods use all of the grain, and so contain more fiber than white rice and refined flour.

Whole grain and refined foods

Whole grain flour is ground from whole grains of wheat and is made into whole grain bread, whole grain pasta, and other whole grain products. Most white flour, pasta, and white bread is made from wheat from which much of the fiber has been removed. All bread and pasta, however, contains some fiber.

BROWN BREAD OR WHOLE GRAIN?

Most whole grain breads are brown, but not all brown breads are whole grain. You have to look at the packaging to see how much fiber a loaf of bread contains.

Food with no fiber

Many foods contain almost no fiber at all. Milk and other dairy products, meat, and fish contain no natural fiber. Many other foods, such as chocolate, soda drinks, some cookies, and cakes, have had all or nearly all the fiber taken out.

What Happens in the Digestive System?

The job of the digestive system is to break up the nutrients in food into pieces that are small enough to pass through the walls of the digestive tract and into the bloodstream. Carbohydrates, fats, and proteins are broken down into separate **molecules**, and even, in the case of protein, into parts of molecules. Water molecules are so small they pass easily into the blood, but with fiber the opposite is true. It cannot be broken down small enough, and so is not absorbed and passes through the digestive system.

In the mouth

Digestion begins in the mouth. The teeth slice, chop, and grind the food into smaller pieces that mix with saliva to make a soft mush. Chewing is particularly important in breaking up fiber. It makes the fiber soft and easy to swallow. When the mouthful of food has been chewed enough, your tongue pushes it to the back of your mouth, and you automatically swallow it.

In the stomach

The mushy pulp passes down your throat, through the **pharynx**, and into the **esophagus**, the tube that joins your mouth to your stomach. The walls of the stomach make a strong acid called hydrochloric acid. This acid usually kills off any germs in the food and starts to break the proteins up into separate molecules. Your stomach is a stretchy bag that stores and churns the food for a few hours. The mushy pulp gradually changes into a kind of thick soup called **chyme**. Every so often, some of the chyme squirts from your stomach into the small intestine.

Body fact

In adults, the length of the digestive tube from the mouth to the anus is about 9.5 meters (31 feet) long. That is as long as about five grown men lined up in a row head to toe. In children it is shorter.

In the small intestine

The small intestine is a long thin tube. As chyme passes into the tube, it mixes with digestive juices that come from the **liver**, the **pancreas**, and the walls of the small intestine. The juice from the pancreas **neutralizes** the acid of the stomach juice. This lets the enzymes in all the digestive juices get to work on the food, breaking up the carbohydrates, proteins, and fats. Gradually these nutrients pass through the walls of the small intestine into the blood. The remainder, mainly fiber, digestive juices, and water, passes from the small intestine into a wider tube called the large intestine.

 The digestive system breaks up food using mechanical and chemical processes. It changes the food from a bite-sized chunk of, for example, peanut butter sandwich into a mushy pulp, and then into a soupy liquid.

The digestive system

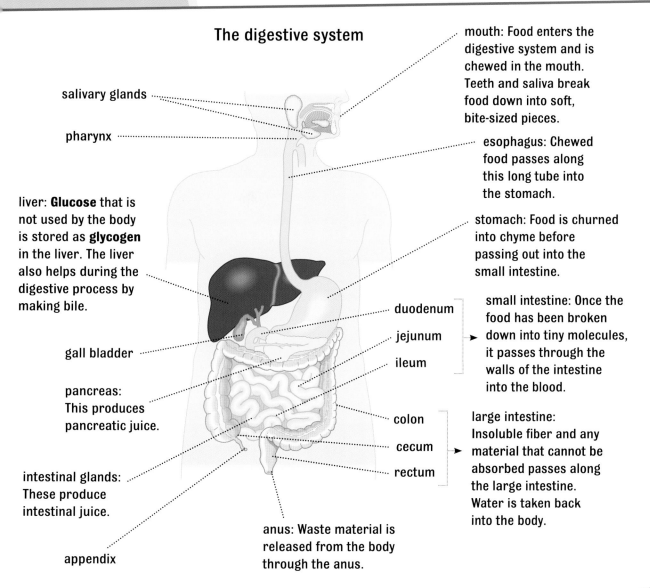

salivary glands

pharynx

liver: **Glucose** that is not used by the body is stored as **glycogen** in the liver. The liver also helps during the digestive process by making bile.

gall bladder

pancreas: This produces pancreatic juice.

intestinal glands: These produce intestinal juice.

appendix

mouth: Food enters the digestive system and is chewed in the mouth. Teeth and saliva break food down into soft, bite-sized pieces.

esophagus: Chewed food passes along this long tube into the stomach.

stomach: Food is churned into chyme before passing out into the small intestine.

duodenum

jejunum

ileum

small intestine: Once the food has been broken down into tiny molecules, it passes through the walls of the intestine into the blood.

colon

cecum

rectum

large intestine: Insoluble fiber and any material that cannot be absorbed passes along the large intestine. Water is taken back into the body.

anus: Waste material is released from the body through the anus.

Digesting Water and Fiber

Water passes easily through the walls of the digestive system into the blood. Some of it is absorbed in the stomach, but more is absorbed in the small intestine. The rest combines with fiber to form a mushy paste that passes into the large intestine. Here more water is absorbed through the walls of the tube, and the paste gradually becomes more solid.

Fiber in the small intestine

Carbohydrates are broken up in the mouth, in the stomach, and in the small intestine. Fiber, however, is not able to be digested and absorbed in the small intestine and passes largely unchanged into the large intestine.

Fiber in the large intestine

The undigested fiber travels slowly through the large intestine and forms one of the main components of feces. Feces, however, is not simply fiber and water. It also contains digestive juices, mucus, dead cells from the walls of the digestive system, and bacteria from the large intestine.

The wall of the small intestine is lined with tiny bumps called villi. The villi provide a bigger surface area for absorbing nutrients.

Hostile environment

The digestive system is a hostile and harsh environment. The enzymes and acid in the juices, which break down food so efficiently, can also attack the living cells of the digestive system itself. The walls of the stomach and intestines are protected by mucus. The lining of the stomach and intestine have a rapid turnover of cells, which means the cells only last a few days. As the cells die, they join the undigested waste.

Water

As water is absorbed through the lining of the stomach and intestine, it can carry with it water-soluble vitamins and minerals. More water is absorbed in the large intestine. As long as the body is not short of water, enough remains in the large intestine to make the feces soft and moist.

 This high magnification scan shows the mucus lining of the large intestine. Mucus helps the feces move and protects the wall of the intestine from damage.

Getting rid of feces

Of all the food you eat, only a small fraction completes the whole journey through the digestive system. Feces are stored at the end of the large intestine. It moves from there into the rectum and is then expelled from the body through the anus. A tight muscle in the anus relaxes to allow the feces to pass through.

TIME IN TRANSIT

Most undigested food takes about 10 hours to reach the large intestine. It may take up to another 20 hours before it finally leaves the body.

Using Fiber

Most fiber is insoluble fiber. It is not digested and passes through the intestines with all the other waste matter. Fiber makes the waste matter, called feces, bulkier. Bulky feces helps the large intestine (also called the bowel) to work better and helps to keep it healthy. Some fiber is soluble.

A long and winding journey

The small intestine is coiled within the folds of the large intestine. Food has to make its way through all the coils into the large intestine. Undigested food and waste then have to travel upward—against **gravity**—along and down to reach the anus, the final exit. The process by which food and waste are moved through the digestive tubes is called peristalsis.

Peristalsis

The walls of the digestive tract contain circular bands of muscles. When a band of muscle contracts, it pushes the food forward. At the same time, the band of muscle in front of the food relaxes, allowing the food to slide through it. The movement of each muscle relaxing and then contracting passes along the tube like a wave. The muscles in the small intestines work continually, churning the food around the tube, but the muscles in the large intestine work much more slowly.

Peristalsis fact

Peristalsis moves food through the digestive system no matter what position your body is in. This means that even if you are upside-down, you can still digest food.

Healthy bowels

If you eat plenty of fiber and drink plenty of water, you are likely to empty your bowels about once a day. This keeps the muscles of the large intestine healthy and helps keep a healthy balance of bacteria in the bowel. Some people go to the bathroom more often, and some people go less often than once a day. What matters most is that the waste material is bulky and easy to push out of the body.

Absorbing cholesterol

Oats and certain fruits and vegetables contain soluble fiber. Soluble fiber can bind to bile acids that are released into the small intestine to help digest fat. These bile acids cannot then be reabsorbed. Instead they pass into the large intestine, where they form part of the feces. This means that more stored cholesterol in the blood has to be used to make new bile acids. This is how soluble fiber in the diet helps to lower blood cholesterol levels.

Food moves through all the tubes in the digestive system in much the same way as you squeeze toothpaste out of a tube. Valves separate one stage of the digestive system from the next. They allow food to travel only in one direction—unless you are vomiting!

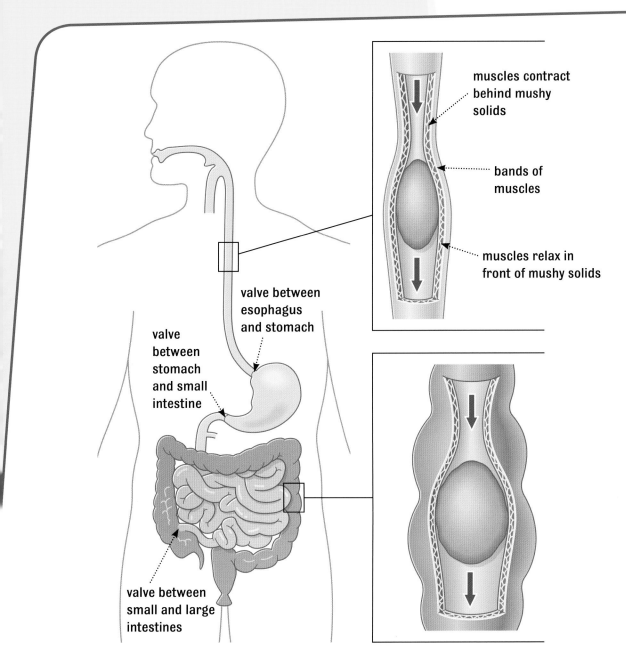

muscles contract behind mushy solids

bands of muscles

muscles relax in front of mushy solids

valve between esophagus and stomach

valve between stomach and small intestine

valve between small and large intestines

Water in the Body

Water is the main ingredient of all the different fluids in the body, including digestive juices, blood, sweat, and urine. Each of these liquids needs water to make them runny. In addition, all the organs and tissues inside your body are coated with moisture. Salty water inside and outside the cells allows nutrients and chemicals to enter and leave each cell. Water is also involved in many of the chemical reactions that take place inside the body.

Digestive juices

Digestive juices, produced in the liver and pancreas, trickle through narrow tubes and into the small intestine. They join other digestive juices made in the mouth, stomach, and in the walls of the intestines.

Hitching a ride

Minerals, such as salt, and some vitamins can only be taken into the body along with water. They dissolve in water and pass with it into the blood.

Blood

The clear, watery part of blood is called plasma. This clear liquid has sugar and other nutrients dissolved in it. Red blood cells take in oxygen in the lungs. As the blood circulates around the body, every living cell is provided with a constant supply of food and oxygen.

» Drinking plenty of water helps to keep your skin moist and healthy. It also helps all the cells in your body work better.

Water in the cells

Water plays an important role in helping nutrients and oxygen pass from the blood into each cell. Chemical reactions inside the cells change glucose and oxygen into energy, while other reactions allow the cell to carry out its own particular tasks. Many of these chemical reactions involve water. Water then helps carbon dioxide and waste chemicals pass from the cell into the blood to be taken away and expelled from the body.

Urine and sweat

Waste chemicals are carried away from the cells by the blood and leave the body in urine or sweat. Urine is made in the kidneys (see pages 26 and 27), while sweat is made in the sweat glands and is pumped out of the body through tiny holes in the skin. Although you are only aware of sweating when you are very hot or the air is very moist, you are actually sweating all the time. Sweat consists mainly of water with salt and other waste chemicals dissolved in it.

Water fact

Your body makes 10 liters (21 pints) of digestive juices every day. Most of this is water that is reabsorbed into the body.

Nearly two-thirds of your body is water. Some parts of the body contain more water than other parts. This chart shows the percentage of water in different parts of the body.

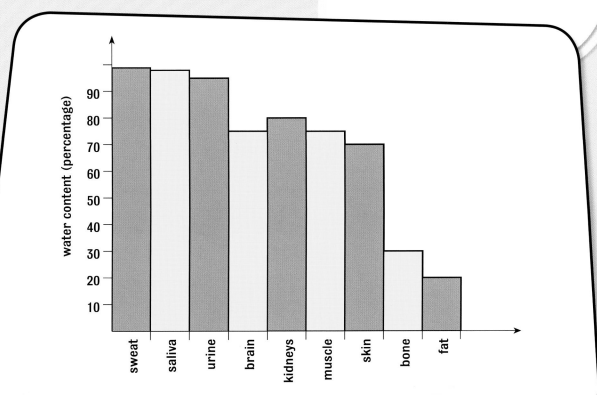

Water Balance

Your body loses water all the time. It loses water just from breathing, but it loses most water in the form of urine and sweat. Altogether, you probably lose about 1 to 2 liters (2.1 to 4.2 pints) of water a day, depending on the weather and how active you are. To replace the water lost, you take in new supplies of water every day in your food and by drinking. Your body has to balance the water lost with the water taken in.

Urine

Nearly half of all the water you lose is urine. How much urine your kidneys make depends on how much water you have drunk and how hot the weather is. The more you drink, the more urine you make. However, when you are hot, you lose more water as sweat. To keep the amount of water in your body balanced, your kidneys then produce less urine.

Sweating

Your body loses water through the skin all the time, but when you are hot you sweat much more. Sweating helps to cool your body down. The water is pumped onto your skin, but the heat of your body makes it evaporate. As it evaporates it takes heat from your blood.

Breathing out

When blood reaches your lungs, carbon dioxide and water **vapor** pass from the blood into the lungs. These two gases then leave the body with the air that you breathe out. Every day you breathe out 500 milliliters (1 pint) of water in the form of vapor.

》 If you breathe out onto a mirror, the mirror will mist up with water droplets. These droplets have **condensed** from water vapor in the air that you have just breathed out.

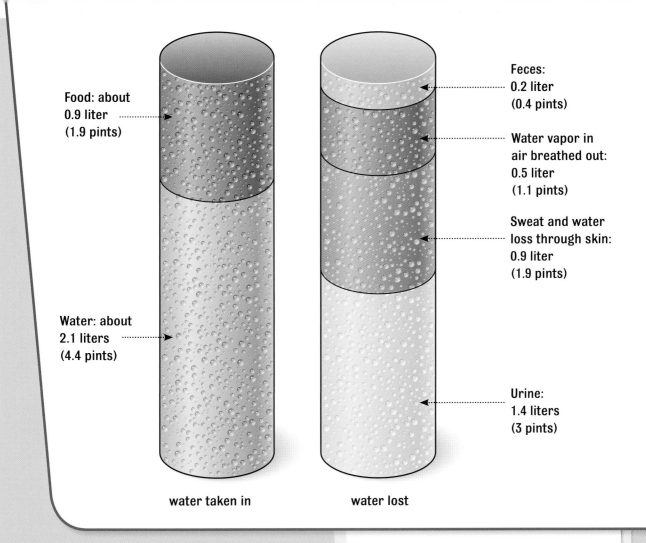

Food: about
0.9 liter
(1.9 pints)

Water: about
2.1 liters
(4.4 pints)

Feces:
0.2 liter
(0.4 pints)

Water vapor in
air breathed out:
0.5 liter
(1.1 pints)

Sweat and water
loss through skin:
0.9 liter
(1.9 pints)

Urine:
1.4 liters
(3 pints)

water taken in

water lost

Feces

Feces contains water as well as fiber and waste materials. The water in feces makes it soft and easier to push out of the body. Usually only about 6 percent of the body's water is lost through feces. If you have **diarrhea**, however, a lot of extra water and salts may be lost. It is important to drink extra water to make up for any lost while suffering from diarrhea.

Thirst

Thirst is a strong signal that your body needs more water to balance the water lost. You feel thirsty when your mouth becomes drier because it is making less saliva. By this time, your body is really short of water. You should drink regularly throughout the day, so that your body does not have to send you this emergency signal!

 These tanks show how the amounts of water you take in and lose are made up. The more water you drink, the more you will lose as urine. This means the amount of water in your body stays about the same.

Water in the Kidneys

You have two kidneys, one on each side of the body just above your waist. They filter the blood and remove poisonous waste, such as **urea**, and excess water and salt. The water with salt and urea dissolved in it trickles from the kidneys down to the bladder, where it is stored.

Poisonous waste

The main ingredient of urea is **nitrogen**. The liver changes the body's waste nitrogen into urea, a solid that dissolves easily in the water in the blood. The liver also breaks down other poisons in the body and turns them into harmless waste chemicals. These include chemicals that you would not usually think of as poisons, such as caffeine in cola.

In the kidneys

Each kidney is made up of over a million tiny filters called nephrons. As blood enters a filter, water and everything dissolved in it is forced out of the blood. Most of the water and all the dissolved food and nutrients pass through the filter and back into the blood. What remains is excess water with urea, salt, and waste chemicals dissolved in it. It is called urine, and it moves down one of the tubes, called a ureter, into the bladder.

About a quarter of your blood passes through your kidneys every minute. The kidneys clean the blood by filtering out poisonous chemicals and excess salt and water. This produces urine, which is stored in the bladder.

vein carries purified blood back to heart

artery brings blood to kidneys

nephrons filter blood

kidney

kidney

ureter

ureter carries urine to bladder

bladder

urethra

Excess water

You may think that drinking extra water will make your kidneys work harder, but in fact extra water makes it easier for your kidneys. The more water there is in your blood, the more diluted the excess salt and other wastes become. This means that each filter has to deal with less salt and waste.

Urine

The kidneys send a constant trickle of urine into the bladder, where it is stored. As the bladder fills up with urine, it stretches. Nerves in the walls of the bladder alert your brain when you need to urinate. If you wait until your bladder is very full, the need to urinate will become desperate. The more liquid you drink, the more often you need to urinate.

Urinating

A ring of muscle at the bottom of the bladder usually keeps the bladder tightly closed. When you urinate, this muscle relaxes and urine flows out of your body from the bladder through a tube called the urethra.

Bladder fact

Your bladder can hold only about 0.5 liter (1.1 pints) of urine at a time, but your body makes about three times this amount every day. This means that you have to urinate several times a day.

 Babies cannot recognize when they need to urinate and cannot control the muscle that allows urine to leave the bladder. They wear diapers to absorb the urine instead.

Too Little Water

If you do not drink enough water, you become dehydrated. This makes it difficult for your body to get rid of the poisonous waste chemicals in your blood. If you do not drink enough for many hours, you will become thirstier and thirstier as your body becomes increasingly desperate for water. People can survive for only a few days without water.

Dehydration

You do not always feel symptoms of mild dehydration, but as you become more dehydrated you begin to feel thirsty. If you do not drink you can begin to feel tired and dizzy. Dehydration can cause headaches and a dry mouth.

Sweating

Sweating also causes dehydration, so you should always drink more liquid in hot weather or when you are in a hot place. People who are exercising vigorously can lose up to 1.7 liters (3.6 pints) of sweat an hour and are particularly in danger of dehydration.

Severe dehydration

When people suffer from severe dehydration, all of the tissues in their body become short of water and cannot function properly. The heart starts to beat very fast and the **blood pressure** falls. If they do not get treatment they will go into **shock** and die.

 Tennis players often have to play hard in very hot weather. Players sip water during the breaks between games so they will not become dehydrated.

Dying of thirst

When you think of someone dying of thirst, you probably think of people stranded at sea or lost in the desert, but millions of people worldwide die of dehydration every year. Most of these deaths are due to dysentery, an infectious disease that causes severe diarrhea. Other people die of dehydration when they lose a lot of blood or suffer burns that cover a large area of their body.

This person is very sick. She has been given an IV with a mixture of water, glucose, and salts. It is fed into her blood to stop her from becoming dehydrated.

ANNALISE'S STORY

Annalise drank very little during the day, because she didn't like using the school bathrooms. Her skin was dry, she often had headaches, and felt tired and listless. Then she read on the Internet that these problems could be caused by dehydration. She carried a bottle of water to drink during the day. When she got home, she drank lots of water. Her headaches have gone, she now feels more energetic, and her skin is no longer dry.

Too Much Water

In normal circumstances it is quite difficult to drink too much water. When you have drunk about 1 liter (2.1 pints), your stomach will be full and you will not want to drink any more. The people who are most likely to drink too much water are those who are trying to avoid dehydration. When people become overheated, they may overcorrect and drink far too much liquid. Too much water upsets the balance of water and salt in the body and, in extreme cases, can cause death.

Balancing water and salt

Salt controls how much water passes out of the blood into your tissues to keep them moist. Your kidneys normally make sure that your blood contains the right amount of salt and water. But if the blood contains too much water and not enough salt, water leaves the blood and floods the tissues of the body.

Overheating

Athletes and, more dangerously, people who take the illegal drug ecstasy are most at risk of overheating. When you become hot, your body sweats to cool you down. Sweat includes salt and water, so when you sweat your body loses both. Sweating usually keeps your temperature more or less constant, but sometimes people become so hot that sweating cannot cool them. Highly trained athletes should know how much water they need to drink to prevent overheating, but the drug ecstasy makes people think that everything is all right with the world, even when things are going dangerously wrong.

 Drinking water usually helps your kidneys to work better, but, if your kidneys cannot cope with it, excess water may flood your body.

Flooded with water

Several ecstasy users have died from drinking too much water when they were overheated. Ecstasy users are in danger of becoming dehydrated. However, if they drink huge amounts of water, the amount of salt in the body becomes too diluted. The drug ecstasy also stops the kidneys from working. Instead of the extra water being extracted from the blood, it floods the body's tissues. Most damaging, the brain becomes swollen. As it swells, it is crushed by the bony skull that usually protects it. Pressure on the brain quickly leads to **coma** and death.

Safe amount to drink

Athletes, and anyone who is exercising vigorously or likely to become very hot, should drink about half a liter (1.1 pints) an hour. Sipping water or soft drinks will replace the water lost. Isotonic drinks, which are special drinks for athletes, are the best things to sip, because they include salts.

The effects of ecstasy and too much water in the body can have tragic consequences.

Too Little Fiber

If you do not eat enough fiber, your large intestine will work slowly and sluggishly. This may lead to constipation, which is difficulty in passing feces. Over a long period of time, continual constipation leads to hemorrhoids and possibly cancer of the large intestine.

Moving along

Fiber and food pass into the bowel (another name for the large intestine). Undigested food only moves through the bowel when the muscles of the tube tighten behind it and push it forward. The less undigested food there is in the large intestine, the less often the muscles contract. This means that undigested food stays in the bowel for much longer than it should.

These foods contain almost no fiber. Only the tomato contains a little fiber. If you like to eat food like this, you should also include foods that are high in fiber, such as whole grain bread and vegetables.

Constipation

How easy it is to push feces out of the body depends on how much fiber and water the feces contain. The longer the mushy paste stays in the bowel, the more water from it is absorbed back into the body. This means that the waste material becomes dry and hard, which makes it difficult and painful to push it out of the body.

Testing transit time

Transit time is the time taken for undigested food to pass through your body. It should be between 12 and 24 hours. If it is more than 24 hours, you need to eat more fiber and drink more water.

Hemorrhoids

Constipation is unpleasant and can build up trouble for the future. Adults who often suffer from constipation may develop hemorrhoids. The blood vessels in the anus and rectum become stretched and swollen, like varicose veins. Hemorrhoids are itchy and painful, particularly when passing feces.

Cancer of the bowel

Continual constipation over many years can lead to cancer of the bowel. People who live in North America, Europe, and Australia are more likely to get cancer of the bowel than people who live in Africa and Asia. This may be because most Africans and Asians have far more fiber in their diets.

Eating meals that contain plenty of fiber keeps the large intestine healthy and working well.

Too Much Fiber

Fiber in your diet makes your digestive system work more efficiently. Eating more fiber than you are used to can cause excess gas to build up, causing you to pass gas and even have diarrhea. Too much fiber can also stop you from getting enough nutrients if it fills your stomach and stops you from eating more nutritious food. Some fiber actually prevents particular minerals from being absorbed into the blood.

Gas in the large intestine

Adults normally have about 200 milliliters (0.4 pint) of gases in the digestive system, but children have a bit less. These gases come from various sources. Some of them are produced in the large intestine. There, billions of bacteria produce **methane**, carbon dioxide, and hydrogen as they feed on the undigested food. These gases have a foul smell and may be passed as gas or come out when you go to the bathroom.

Indigestion

Fiber is difficult to digest, so if you eat a lot of it, your system may be unable to digest it all, giving you indigestion. More undigested food in the large intestine gives the bacteria there more to feed on, and so they produce more gas. Some foods, such as beans, cabbage, cauliflower, onions, and garlic, make more gas than others. The extra gases fill the digestive tube, making your **abdomen** sore and swollen. Chewing your food for longer helps to prevent indigestion and reduces excess gas.

This girl has just eaten a meal that contained too much fiber. Now her abdomen is sore because her intestines are swollen with gas.

Irritable digestion

Too much fiber can make your digestive tubes inflamed and irritable. Apart from causing pain, food is pushed through the intestines too quickly, so there is not enough time for the water to be absorbed through the wall of the large intestine into the blood. Extra water in the feces makes it very loose and runny, producing diarrhea.

Replacing nutrients

Young children in particular should not eat too much fiber, because it might replace nutritious food. It fills their stomach so that they stop eating before they have taken in enough carbohydrates, fats, proteins, and other nutrients.

Minerals

The fiber contained in the outer skins of whole grain cereals prevents some minerals, particularly calcium, iron, and zinc, from being absorbed into the blood. Children in particular should not eat a lot of raw bran.

GAS IN THE STOMACH

Most of the gas in your stomach is air that you swallow with your food. It can also include carbon dioxide from carbonated drinks. If there is too much gas in your stomach, you usually burp to get rid of some of it.

Intestines can become inflamed and cause discomfort if the wrong amount of fiber is eaten.

Healthy Eating

Just as it is important to eat enough, but not too much, fiber, it is also important to eat enough, but not too much, of each kind of nutrient— carbohydrates, proteins, fats, vitamins, and minerals. Eating the right amount of all these kinds of foods means you have a balanced diet.

The "MyPyramid" food pyramid

Different kinds of foods are rich in different nutrients. The "MyPyramid" food pyramid divides food into five main groups, plus oils. It shows the kinds of food you should eat most of, and the kinds you should only eat a little of.

1 – Grains

These foods are rich in carbohydrates and so give you energy. If you choose whole grain bread, pasta, and flour, you will get lots of fiber, too. Oatmeal is a breakfast cereal that contains a good quantity of fiber. Eat about 140 grams (5 ounces) from the grains group a day.

2 – Vegetables

Vegetables are rich in vitamins, minerals, and fiber. Eat at least 2 cups of vegetables a day. All types of vegetables count toward this amount.

3 – Fruits

Fruits are also rich in vitamins, minerals, and fiber. Eat at least 1.5 cups of fruits a day.

4 – Milk

The milk group includes milk as well as cheese and yogurt. These foods are rich in protein, vitamins, and minerals (particularly calcium), although many contain quite a lot of fat and no fiber. Eat or drink about 3 cups a day from this group.

5 – Meat and beans

Foods in this group include meat, poultry, fish, eggs, nuts, and pulses. These foods are all rich in protein, but, apart from pulses, they contain no fiber. Nevertheless, protein is very important, particularly for children who are still growing. Eat about 120 to 150 grams (4 to 5 ounces) a day.

Oils

The oils group includes cooking oils such as canola oil. Foods that are high in oil include mayonnaise, olives, nuts, and seeds. Oils contain essential nutrients, so some are good in the diet. However, people should limit their intake because oils are often high in calories.

 The "MyPyramid" shows the wide variety of food you should eat to enjoy a balanced diet. It is divided into five main groups of food, plus oils. The space given to each reflects how much of each you should eat.

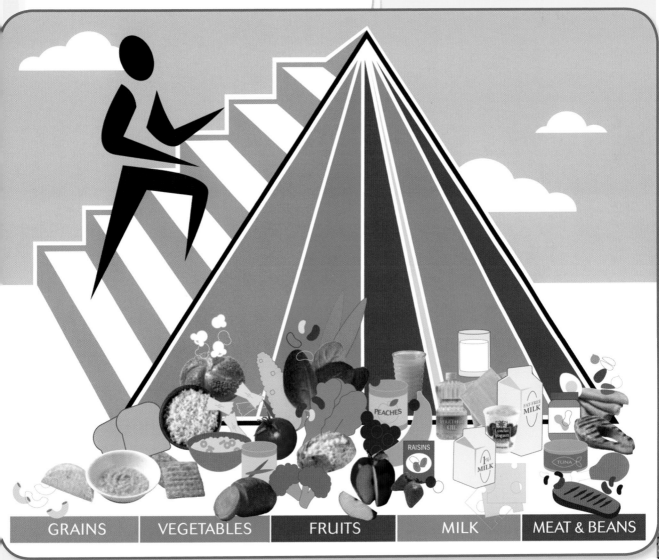

GRAINS | VEGETABLES | FRUITS | MILK | MEAT & BEANS

Healthy Drinking

Most people lose about 1.2 liters (2.5 pints) of water a day, mostly in the form of urine and sweat. You need to take in enough water to replace the amount lost. Your body gets nearly a third of the water it needs from food, but the rest must come from drinks. This means that most people should drink about 6 to 8 glasses of fluids a day.

Water in food and drinks

If you follow the "MyPyramid" food pyramid, you will absorb water from the fruits and vegetables you eat every day, as well as from bread, pasta, rice, and potatoes. All food has some water in it, otherwise it would be too dry to eat.

This girl is enjoying a slice of watermelon. It contains a lot of juice and will help to replace some of the water she loses during the day.

Soup and all drinks are mainly water. Some, such as tea, are made by adding water, but others, such as milk, are already made mainly of water. You can replace the liquid your body loses by drinking fruit juices and milk, but it is particularly helpful to your body if you also drink plain water.

Caffeine

Cola, tea, and coffee all contain a substance called caffeine. Caffeine speeds up the processes in the body and makes you feel more alert. It also makes your kidneys produce more urine, so they extract more water from your blood. Most people can tolerate a certain amount of caffeine without becoming dehydrated. However, when you consume more caffeine than you are used to, this can cause mild dehydration.

Alcohol

Alcohol in large amounts can be dehydrating. People who have drunk a lot of alcohol often suffer from a hangover afterward. Their mouth feels dry, their head may ache, and they may feel tired and sick. Most of these symptoms are caused by dehydration—just one of many problems caused by drinking alcohol.

Men should drink no more than two drinks a day without causing a major risk to their health. Women should drink no more than one drink a day. A drink is defined as 355 milliliters (12 ounces) of regular beer (one bottle); a 148-milliliter (5-ounce) glass of wine; or 44 milliliters (1.5 ounces) of distilled spirits. Pregnant women should not drink alcohol at all.

The bottle of water shows you how much liquid you should drink every day. The glasses show one way of drinking this amount of liquid. Remember that you cannot count cola, tea, or coffee.

Healthy Diets

Your diet consists of all the foods you usually eat. Many people in western countries, including North America, Europe, and Australia, eat a diet that is too low in fiber. People from other parts of the world eat food that usually contains much more fiber. Vegetarians and vegans follow special diets, but these diets usually contain plenty of fiber.

Traditional diets

Most people in Western countries use flour refined from wheat, but people in Africa, Asia, and South America often make flour from other grains, such as maize and rice, and this flour is less refined. Their diets often include beans, peas, or lentils, which are cheap and rich in nutrients and fiber. Traditional recipes from these areas are becoming more popular, as people realize how healthy and tasty they are.

Vegetarian and vegan diets

Vegetarians do not eat meat and often do not eat fish, either. Vegans exclude any food that has come from animals, including milk and all other dairy food. Vegetarian diets may be more healthy than meat diets because they are more likely to be high in fiber and low in fat. Vegan diets are also usually rich in fiber, but vegans have to choose their food carefully to make sure they get all the nutrients they need.

These children are enjoying couscous, a traditional meal from North Africa. It includes chickpeas and meat in a spicy sauce and is served with semolina, a grain that is rich in fiber.

BEN'S STORY

Ben liked to eat chips, fries, burgers, and chocolate, but his doctor told him that he was getting too overweight. Ben changed his diet. He stopped eating such fatty food and ate whole wheat bread and spaghetti instead. The fiber in the food stopped him from feeling hungry. He also drank plenty of water to help make him feel full. When he wanted a snack he had a banana, apple, or raw carrot. He joined a sports club at school. He became fitter and healthy, and soon lost all the excess weight.

People who are sick

People who are sick often do not feel like eating very much. It is, however, particularly important that they do not stop drinking. If you are vomiting or suffering from diarrhea, you need to drink plenty of water or other fluids to replace the extra water lost. Similarly, if you have a high temperature, or a fever, you need to drink plenty of extra water to replace all the water lost through sweating.

When you have a high temperature or a sore throat, you may not feel like eating very much, but it is very important that you drink plenty of water.

Daily Requirements

In Western countries most people eat about 12 grams (0.4 ounce) of fiber a day, but scientists recommend that adults should have a lot more. It is recommended that males 9 to 13 years old should have 31 grams (1.1 ounces) a day, while females in the same age group should have 26 grams (0.7 ounce) a day. Young children should have less fiber. While adults should drink about 6 to 8 glasses of liquid a day, you can reduce this amount if you weigh less than an average adult. Check with your healthcare provider to find the perfect amount for you.

Food		Amount that gives 10 g (0.4 oz) of fiber
Fruits	Apples	3–4 apples
	Bananas	3 bananas
	Oranges	3 oranges
Vegetables	Broccoli	1 large head
	Cabbage	1 medium cabbage
	Carrots	5 carrots
Pulses	Baked beans	1 small can
	Lentils (cooked)	125 grams (0.6 cup)
	Peas (boiled)	200 grams (1 cup)
Cereals	Cornflakes	10 cups
	Oat cakes	10 cakes
	White bread	15 slices
	Whole wheat bread	5 slices
Potatoes	Baked potato	1 large
	Boiled potatoes	7 potatoes

Amount of fiber and water in different foods

Food	Amount of fiber in 100 g (3.5 oz)	Amount of water in 100 g (3.5 oz)
Apples, including skin	1.8 g	85 mL (2.9 oz)
Baked beans	3.7 g	72 mL (2.4 oz)
Bananas	3.4 g	75 mL (2.5 oz)
Boiled egg	0 g	75 mL (2.5 oz)
Cheddar cheese	0 g	36 mL (1.2 oz)
Chocolate (most)	0 g	0.9 mL (0.03 oz)
Cooked white spaghetti	1.2 g	73.8 mL (2.5 oz)
Corn flakes	2.5 g	3 mL (0.1 oz)
Cucumber	0.6 g	96 mL (3.2 oz)
Fish	0 g	65–75 mL (2.2–2.5 oz)
Meat	0 g	40–70 mL (1.4–2.4 oz)
Baked chips	2 g	59 mL (2 oz)
Peanut butter	5.4 g	1 mL (0.03 oz)
Peas	4.7 g	78 mL (2.6 oz)
Plain sponge cake	0.9 g	20 mL (0.7 oz)
Raw tomatoes	1 g	93 mL (3.1 oz)
Semi-skimmed (2%) milk	0 g	90 mL (3 oz)
White bread	2.5 g	37 mL (1.3 oz)
Whole wheat bread	7 g	38 mL (1.3 oz)

This meal contains 7.3 grams (0.26 ounce) of fiber and 289 grams (10 ounces) of water. (That is 289 milliliters of water.)

Glossary

abdomen   belly, the part of the body that contains the stomach and small intestines

amino acid   building block of protein. Different amino acids combine together to form a protein.

artery   tube that carries blood from the heart to different parts of the body

bacteria   single, living cells. Most kinds of bacteria are harmless, but some kinds can cause disease.

blood pressure   pressure the blood puts on the walls of blood vessels as it is pumped around the body. Blood pressure changes depending on the force of the heartbeat.

calcium   simple substance found in the earth and in foods such as milk and cheese. Your body needs calcium for strong, healthy bones and teeth.

carbohydrate   substance in food that your body uses to provide energy. Foods that contain a lot of carbohydrates include bread, rice, potatoes, and sugar.

carbon dioxide   one of the gases in air. Plants take in carbon dioxide to make food and they produce oxygen as a result, one of the things that humans need to survive.

cell   smallest living unit. The body is made up of many different kinds of cells, such as bone cells, blood cells, and skin cells.

cellulose   substance that the walls of plants cells are made of

cholesterol   substance made by the body and found in some foods. It is necessary for certain functions of the body, but can lead to health problems if too much cholesterol is formed and deposited on the walls of blood vessels.

chyme   mushy liquid that passes from the stomach to the small intestine. It is formed from partly digested food mixed with the digestive juices of the stomach.

coma   state of deep sleep from which the patient cannot wake up. Comas can continue for a long time.

condensed   when a gas or a vapor, such as water vapor, cools and changes into a liquid

dehydrated   when the body has less water than it needs

diarrhea   feces that are loose and watery

digest   process of breaking down food when it is eaten. Digestion starts in the mouth when you bite and chew food and continues until the molecules that make up food are taken into the bloodstream.

dissolve   when a solid or gas merges with a liquid

element   simple substance that cannot be broken up into any other substances

energy   ability to do work or to make something happen

enzyme   substance that helps a chemical change take place faster without being changed itself

esophagus   tube through which food travels from the mouth to the stomach

evaporate   when a solid or a liquid becomes a gas

fat   substance that the body can change into energy. A layer of fat under the skin helps to keep the body warm.

feces   undigested food, bacteria, digestive juices, and dead cells that are excreted as solid waste

ferment   to convert sugar to carbon dioxide and alcohol, usually with yeast

fungi   group of living things that includes mushrooms, yeasts, and molds

glucose   type of sugar

glycogen   name for any glucose stored in the liver and muscles following absorption. Extra glucose is stored if it is not needed immediately by the body.

gravity   way that everything is attracted downward, toward the ground

hydrogen   invisible gas that is one of the gases in the air. Hydrogen combines with other substances to form, for example, water, sugar, proteins, and fats.

insoluble fiber   fiber that is unable to dissolve in a liquid

iron   simple substance found in the earth. Your body needs iron so that red blood cells can carry oxygen.

large intestine   part of the intestines through which undigested food passes after it has left the small intestine

liver   body organ that produces digestive juices

methane   gas that occurs naturally in the earth and is made in the body in the large intestine

mineral   non-living substance found in the ground. Your body needs certain minerals to function healthily.

molecule   smallest part of a substance that can exist and still be that substance

mucus   slimy liquid made in the body

neutralize   make something neutral—that is, neither acid nor alkaline

nitrogen   invisible gas that is the main gas in the air. Nitrogen combines with other substances in all the different tissues in your body.

nutrient   part of food that your body needs to get energy, to build and repair cells, and for the cells to function properly. Nutrients include carbohydrates, fats, proteins, vitamins, and minerals.

organ   part of the body that does a particular job. The heart, stomach, and intestines are all organs.

oxygen   one of the invisible gases in air. The body needs oxygen to break down sugar and form energy.

pancreas gland that produces various digestive juices that flow through a tube into the small intestine

pharynx part of the throat where the tubes to the nose, lungs, and stomach begin

phosphorus simple substance that is needed for plants to grow

pollutants substances that cause harm to the environment

protein complex chemical that the body needs to grow and repair cells

pulse part of a food group that includes lentils, peas, and beans. Pulses are the seeds of some plants and are rich in protein.

recycled reused, sometimes in another form

saliva watery liquid made by glands in your mouth and the inside of your cheeks

sediment solid particle that collects at the bottom of a container of liquid

shock condition caused by a fall in blood pressure that can lead to a person becoming unconscious

small intestine part of the intestine into which food passes from the stomach to be digested and absorbed into the blood. Undigested food passes through the small intestine into the large intestine.

soluble fiber fiber that dissolves in water and passes into the blood

urea substance formed from waste material in the liver

urine liquid filtered out of the blood by the kidneys as waste and excreted as a yellowish liquid. Urine consists of urea mixed with excess salt and water.

vapor gas that rises from a liquid or solid

vitamin chemical that your body needs to stay healthy

zinc mineral that the body needs to grow and to help wounds heal

Find Out More

Books

Parker, Steve. *Break It Down: The Digestive System*. Chicago: Raintree, 2007.

Schaefer, Lola, and Ted Schaefer. *What's on Your Plate? Dinner*. Chicago: Raintree, 2006.

Thomas, Isabel. *Real World Data: Graphing Food and Nutrition*. Chicago: Heinemann Library, 2009.

Websites

www.cnpp.usda.gov
This site from the Center for Nutrition Policy and Promotion, a part of the U.S. Department of Agriculture, provides information about health and nutrition. Included is the "MyPyramid" food pyramid, which offers guidelines for a healthy, balanced diet.

www.nutrition.gov
Learn more about nutrition at this educational site set up by the U.S. Department of Agriculture.

www.mckinley.uiuc.edu/Handouts/sports_nutrition.html
This site tells you about drinking fluid and is especially useful if you are an athlete or highly active.

www.mckinley.uiuc.edu/Handouts/high_fiber.htm
This site tells you about fiber and gives examples of the amounts of fiber in different kinds of food.

Index